THIS WALKER BOOK BELONGS TO:

_____

_____

_____

_____

For Max

With thanks to John Barker, B. Vet. Med., M.R.C.V.S.

First published 1982 by Evans Brothers Ltd
First published 1991 by
Walker Books Ltd, 87 Vauxhall Walk
London SE11 5HJ

This edition published 1996

2 4 6 8 10 9 7 5 3

© 1982, 1996 Colin Hawkins

This book has been typeset in Monotype Garamond.

Printed in Hong Kong

British Library Cataloguing in Publication Data
A catalogue record for this book is
available from the British Library.

ISBN 0-7445-4738-5

How to Look After Your

DOG

Colin and Jacqui Hawkins

WALKER BOOKS

AND SUBSIDIARIES

LONDON · BOSTON · SYDNEY

A Dog Is...

A dog is furry with four legs, a tail that wags and a cold wet nose.

"And sharp teeth."

Someone to share the fire with.

"(wag)"

"(wag)"

"I do like fires."

A dog is someone who is able to hear a can being opened from down the end of the garden...

"Sounds like dinner-time."

A dog is someone
who loves you...

Someone
to share the
sofa with.

A dog is someone to bring
your slippers, or the newspapers,
or his favourite old sock,
or his old bone...

"Hello, Daddy!"

"Daddy!"

Choosing Your Dog

A dog is a friend that you can choose – though often he will choose you.

"Da, Da."

Don't take a puppy away from its mother who is too young and hasn't been weaned yet. Puppies are usually weaned at six weeks.

Pick a lively, happy puppy with bright eyes and a glossy coat.

shine
shine
gleam
gleam

Take your new puppy to the vet for advice on vaccines and worming. He will need to be vaccinated at about nine weeks and wormed immediately.

This is to certify that Rover has been inoculated against distemper, hard and soft pad, toad in the hole.

"Is it dinner-time yet?"

When you choose your puppy, try and see the mother to get an idea of how big he will grow. You must choose the right dog for your pocket.

Please help. Large dog to feed.

First Night Home

tick tick tick

On his first night away from his mother a puppy can be lonely. Wrap a hot-water bottle in a blanket and place it in his basket. A ticking clock can also be a comfort.
(Don't forget to switch off the alarm!)

"Whose dinner are you?"

"Hello, sir."

On his first arrival home be careful how your new pup is introduced to older and more established pets, in case they start to get jealous and aggressive.

Even if he is lonely on his first night home, it is not a good idea to allow a pup to sleep on your bed...

This can lead to problems!

Diet

Your puppy should be weaned when you get him. Feed him four small meals a day until he is nine months old, then just one a day at a regular time.

Be careful! Even if he is not hungry, your puppy will love to chew anything from newspapers to carpet slippers. Although dogs enjoy fresh cooked meat and fish, it is fine to buy commercial tinned food.

A balanced diet is more important than a varied diet, but given the chance a dog will eat anything, especially table left-overs (or table left-unders).

Don't feed him raw meat. It will make his breath smell.

"Hello, Rover."

"What a nasty niff!"

Drinking

It is very important that you make sure your dog has fresh water to drink at all times.

Some dogs can also enjoy tea, although tea-drinking dogs are usually found only in the British Isles.

Do not over-feed your dog or you will end up taking him for a roll rather than a walk.

How to recognize an overweight dog

A persistent beggar

"More ... please ... more ... more ... please..."

Excessive dribbling →

A roll of fat on his back

Fatty rounded chest →

You should be able to feel your dog's hips and ribs.

Your dog will get as fat as you allow him.

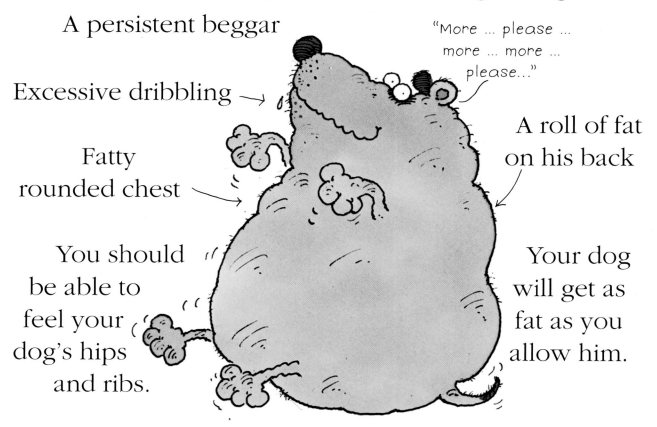

Toilet-training

All dogs need to be toilet-trained. Introduce your pup to his litter-tray on his first day home.

And then encourage the habit of going outside as soon as possible. Praise and reward him when he does the right thing but don't punish him when he gets it wrong.

"I've finished."

When in town, train your dog to use the gutter.

"You dirty dog."

Allowing a dog to foul the pavement is an offence. Dog-fouled pavements are unsightly, a health hazard and can be dangerous.

Pavement Fouler

Don't allow your dog to foul places where children play. This can cause a very serious health hazard.

"Oops, sorry!"

Obedience

It is very important, in order for both
you and your dog to enjoy a happy life together,

that he should be obedient at all times.

"Well ... I did like walkies..."

Obedience Training

"Sit."

"Good boy!"

"Good boy!"

"Sit."

Sit

To teach your dog to "sit", press his tail-end gently but firmly to the ground, at the same time telling him to "sit". When he has sat, praise and reward him.

Stay

When he understands "sit", teach him to "stay" by repeating the commands "sit" and "stay" while slowly backing away from him.

"Hurry up, this grass is wet!"

"Stay ... sit ... stay ... sit ... stay ..."

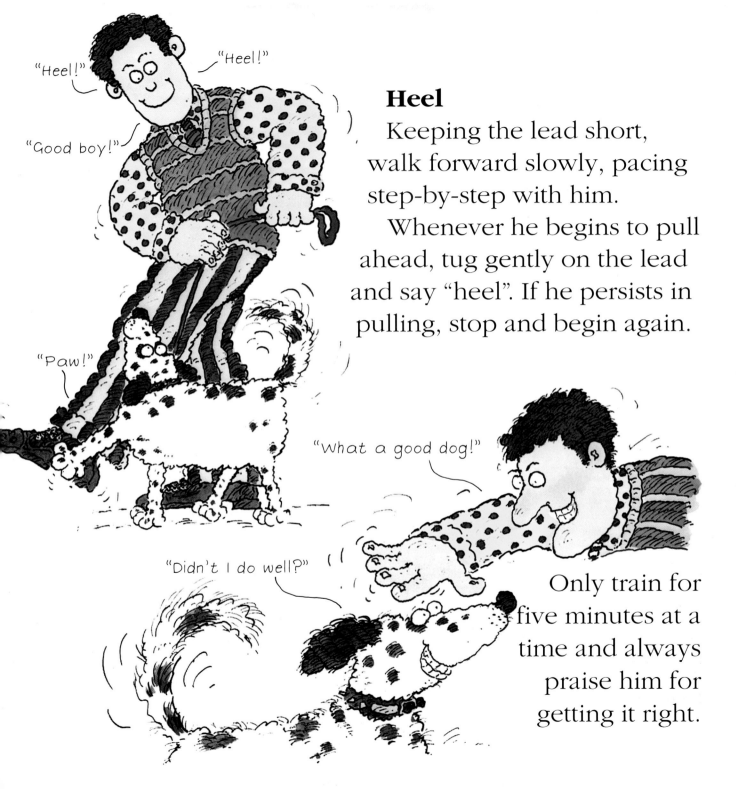

Heel

Keeping the lead short, walk forward slowly, pacing step-by-step with him.

Whenever he begins to pull ahead, tug gently on the lead and say "heel". If he persists in pulling, stop and begin again.

Only train for five minutes at a time and always praise him for getting it right.

Grooming

A dog's fur can at any time be full of fleas, twigs, ants, crumbs, old chewing-gum or grass cuttings. Regular grooming is therefore essential.

Bathing

"Baths are OK once you're in."

Give your dog a bath only when he needs it. If he needs a bath in the winter, make sure that the room is very warm.

After his bath wrap him up in towels and dry him thoroughly. You can also try drying him with a hairdryer.

Breeding
(The patter of tiny paws)

You must decide whether or not you want your dog or bitch to breed. There are several ways of preventing puppies. Ask your vet for advice.

Keep your bitch inside while she is on heat but be prepared for unexpected callers.

"Boo!"

If your bitch is going to have puppies and she begins spending more and more time in dark, quiet places, then the birth of her puppies is very near.

Take care to see that her feeding bowls are close by and that the bed is comfortable and large enough for both her and the puppies. Try to avoid disturbing her and discourage visitors as much as you can.

Habits

A dog is a creature of habit...

He will instinctively
join other dogs and form a hunting pack.

"Hello, pack leader."

"... ?? I thought you
were pack leader!"

When your dog rolls over on his back, or crawls along on
his belly in front of you or another dog, he is instinctively
playing a submissive role to the pack leader.

When he rolls in all the smelliest things he can find it is to camouflage his scent for hunting.

"What do you think of this fantastic camouflage smell, pack leader?"

"Ugh!"

"Round and round the garden..."

"Walkies, Bruce?"

"Ooh yes, please."

"Ooh yes!"

"Oh, I do like walkies!"

He will turn round and round in his basket to tread down the reeds as his ancestors did.

He will also get very excited at being shown his lead, treating it as a signal to work himself up into a pre-hunt fever.

Old Dogs

Old dogs can become hard
of hearing, short-sighted …

"Sit!"

"Yes, I am fit,
thank you."

and forgetful.

An old dog may need
dental treatment
and medication
for arthritis.

"Te ... tum ... te ... tum..."

Don't expect an old dog to walk too far. You may have to carry him home.

"The old legs aren't what they were."

Chop food up as finely as possible and feed him two or three small meals a day.

"Mmm ... beef puree."

Old dogs feel the cold more than young dogs, so keep them warm.

MORE WALKER PAPERBACKS
For You to Enjoy

Also by Colin and Jacqui Hawkins

HOW TO LOOK AFTER YOUR…

Four brilliant pet-care books, packed with information for the young, would-be pet owner.

"A must… There are useful tips on home, feeding, health and much more with fun drawings." *R.S.P.C.A. Animal Action*

How to Look After Your Cat   0-7445-4737-7
How to Look After Your Dog   0-7445-4738-5
How to Look After Your Hamster   0-7445-4379-7
How to Look After Your Rabbit   0-7445-4380-0
£4.50 each

COME FOR A RIDE ON THE GHOST TRAIN

"Every page must be turned with care as a comic, but a wholly scary surprise is revealed under the simplest flaps. Irresistible."
Julia Eccleshare, The Bookseller

0-7445-3671-5   £4.99

TERRIBLE, TERRIBLE TIGER/THE WIZARD'S CAT

Two wonderfully entertaining rhyming picture books about a tiger who is not quite what he seems and a cat who wishes he were something else!

Terrible, Terrible Tiger   0-7445-5230-3   £4.50
The Wizard's Cat   0-7445-5231-1   £4.50

Walker Paperbacks are available from most booksellers, or by post from B.B.C.S., P.O. Box 941, Hull, North Humberside HU1 3YQ
24 hour telephone credit card line 01482 224626

To order, send: Title, author, ISBN number and price for each book ordered, your full name and address, and a cheque or postal order payable to BBCS for the total amount and allow the following for postage and packing:
UK and BFPO: £1.00 for the first book, and 50p for each additional book to a maximum of £3.50.
Overseas and Eire: £2.00 for the first book, £1.00 for the second and 50p for each additional book.
Prices and availability are subject to change without notice.